JOURNALING
TO RECOVERY

My personal reflections using the Twelve-Step Program

Vol._____

ABBEY PRESS

Created by Barbara S. Reznicek
With a foreword by Morton Kelsey

Cover Design:
Scott Wannemuehler

Library of Congress Catalog Number
88-83361

ISBN 0-87029-219-6

Published by Abbey Press
St. Meinrad, Indiana 47577

CONTENTS

FOREWORD

Nearly everyone needs to recover from some personality flaw. Few people live complete, fulfilled lives. The Twelve Steps of Alcoholics Anonymous give a practical method of overcoming addictions and moving toward emotional and spiritual maturity. They offer a discipline that can lead to spiritual transformation.

Not many people get full benefit from any spiritual program without keeping a record of where they have been, what they are doing, and where they wish to go. This book is a journal to help keep that log, to nudge you forward on your spiritual journey.

We do not complete these Twelve Steps simply by going through them once. Like a spiral staircase, we go by the same point again and again, but each time we hope for a higher level. In addition to the Twelve Steps, four additional sections provide help to deal with character defects, character strengths, life goals, and the personal chapters of our lives.

Continuing to keep a personal journal gives more and deeper insights into our journey of recovery and renewal. Only as we date each item in the recovery ledger can we see the kind of progress we make toward realizing our potential. The more we grow, the more opportunity we usually see for further growth.

Why is there a need to keep a permanent written record? There are many reasons for this practice.

1. All of us have faulty memories and we tend to forget those parts of our lives that are uncomfortable to remember. In times of discouragement we can even forget our great experiences of God's caring and of human love.

2. Scheduling a specific time to write in the journal forces us to pause and reflect. Without this kind of reflection, personal transformation is seldom possible. I need a time for reflecting with my journal each day.

3. Dated entries indicate the span of time since we last paused to take stock of ourselves and to make plans for creative change.

4. We cannot change what we do not know about ourselves. The journal is a private place where we express what might be inexpressible to another human being. Writing a personal inventory of mistakes, faults, and wrongs prepares us to take Step Five where we share these failings with another person. Entries in the logbook should carefully reflect on who that person will be.

5. Keeping a journal has little value unless inventory and reflections are totally honest. Addictions—aspects of our lives that

we are unable to control—call for God's help. Addictions appear in limitless forms: alcohol, laziness, pride, dependency, drugs, anger, fear, gluttony, money, security, work, greed, sexual experience, despondency, and even a fear that no higher power cares for us or helps us.

6. Significant dreams can be recorded. God can speak through dreams to reveal hidden parts of ourselves and show new possibilities.

7. Any honest journal is extremely personal and confidential; it should not be left lying around. If entries in the log could injure another who might break confidentiality and read it, these should be written in a personal code.

8. Writing our reflections and personal inventories makes them much more real and substantial. This concrete, written record can help us change whatever needs changing and can stimulate us to develop positive traits.

9. For me, a time of quiet is helpful before I write in my journal. I can center myself, listen to the Holy Spirit, and find which section of the journal needs more reflection and work.

10. The section entitled "Personal Chapters" is a good place to start the story of your life from earliest memories, or to continue your reflections on specific steps. When we write a personal history, our memory usually opens up and heals the past.

11. A journal can become a sacrament of inner spiritual growth and change. My book, *Adventure Inward* (Minneapolis, Minnesota: Augsburg Publishing House, 1980), offers many additional suggestions for keeping a recovery journal. In *Let Go, Let God* (Minneapolis, Minnesota: Augsburg Publishing House, 1985), John Keller provides a remarkable guide for those wishing to explore the spiritual significance of the Twelve Steps of Alcoholics Anonymous.

Morton Kelsey

THE TWELVE STEPS

1. We admitted we were powerless over our addiction—that our lives had become unmanageable.

2. Came to believe that a Power greater than ourselves could restore us to sanity.

3. Made a decision to turn our will and our lives over to the care of God *as we understood Him.*

4. Made a searching and fearless moral inventory of ourselves.

5. Admitted to God, to ourselves, and to another human being the exact nature of our wrongs.

6. Were entirely ready to have God remove all these defects of character.

7. Humbly asked Him to remove our shortcomings.

8. Made a list of all persons we had harmed, and became willing to make amends to them all.

9. Made direct amends to such people wherever possible, except when to do so would injure them or others.

10. Continued to take personal inventory, and when we were wrong promptly admitted it.

11. Sought through prayer and meditation to improve our conscious contact with God *as we understood Him,* praying only for knowledge of His will for us and the power to carry that out.

12. Having had a spiritual awakening as the result of these steps, we tried to carry this message to addicts, and to practice these principles in all our affairs.

The Twelve Steps of Alcoholics Anonymous

1–We admitted we were powerless over alcohol—that our lives had become unmanageable. 2–Came to believe that a Power greater than ourselves could restore us to sanity. 3–Made a decision to turn our will and our lives over to the care of God *as we understood Him.* 4–Made a searching and fearless moral inventory of ourselves. 5–Admitted to God, to ourselves, and to another human being the exact nature of our wrongs. 6–Were entirely ready to have God remove all these defects of character. 7–Humbly asked Him to remove our shortcomings. 8–Made a list of all persons we had harmed, and became willing to make amends to them all. 9–Made direct amends to such people wherever possible, except when to do so would injure them or others. 10–Continued to take personal inventory and when we were wrong, promptly admitted it. 11–Sought through prayer and meditation to improve our conscious contact with God *as we understood Him,* praying only for knowledge of His will for us and the power to carry that out. 12–Having had a spiritual awakening as the result of these steps, we tried to carry this message to alcoholics and to practice these principles in all our affairs.

(The Twelve Steps reprinted for adaptation with permission of Alcoholics Anonymous World Services, Inc.)

STEP ONE

We admitted we were powerless over our addiction—that our lives had become unmanageable.

Continued on page

5

STEP TWO

Came to believe that a Power greater than ourselves could restore us to sanity.

Continued on page

STEP THREE

Made a decision to turn our will and our lives over to the care of God as we understood Him.

Continued on page

STEP FOUR

Made a searching and fearless moral inventory of ourselves.

Continued on page

STEP FIVE

Admitted to God, to ourselves, and to another human being the exact nature of our wrongs.

Continued on page

STEP SIX

Were entirely ready to have God remove all these defects of character.

Continued on page

STEP SEVEN

Humbly asked Him to remove our shortcomings.

Continued on page

STEP EIGHT

Made a list of all persons we had harmed and became willing to make amends to them all.

Continued on page

STEP NINE

Made direct amends to such people wherever possible, except when to do so would injure them or others.

Continued on page

STEP TEN

Continued to take personal inventory, and when we were wrong promptly admitted it.

Continued on page

STEP ELEVEN

Sought through prayer and meditation to improve our conscious contact with God as we understood Him, praying only for knowledge of His will for us and the power to carry that out.

Continued on page

STEP TWELVE

Having had a spiritual awakening as the result of these steps, we tried to carry this message to addicted persons, and to practice these principles in all our affairs.

Continued on page

CHARACTER DEFECTS

Continued on page

CHARACTER STRENGTHS

Continued on page

LIFE GOALS

Continued on page

PERSONAL CHAPTERS

Continued on page